THROUGH THE EYES OF AN

IMMIGRATION ATTORNEY:

Finding Freedom From Divorce While
Maintaining Your Immigration Status

Judith Delus Montgomery, Esq.

Jacobs & Whitehall
21750 Hardy Oak Blvd
Suite 104 – 51700
San Antonio, Texas 78258
(888) 570-7338
www.jacobsandwhitehall.com

Ordering Information:

Quantity sales. Special discounts are available on quantity purchases by corporations, associations, and others. For details, contact the publisher at the address above.

Orders by U.S. trade bookstores and wholesalers. Please contact Jacobs & Whitehall: Tel: (888) 991-2766 or visit www.jacobsandwhitehall.com.

Printed in the United States of America

Published in 2022

ISBN: 978-1-954506-52-7

DEDICATION

This book is dedicated to two very special people in my life. The one that gave me life and that one that I gave life to. You two make my world go round and push me to be the very best version of myself in all I do. This is dedicated to Rose and BJ.

DISCLAIMER

This publication is intended to be used for educational purposes only. No legal advice is being given, and no attorney-client relationship is intended to be created by reading this material. The author assumes no liability for any errors or omissions or for how this book or its contents are used or interpreted, or for any consequences resulting directly or indirectly from the use of this book. For legal or any other advice, please consult an experienced attorney or the appropriate expert, who is aware of the specific facts of your case and is knowledgeable in the law in your jurisdiction.

Atlanta Family & Immigration Law

2860 Church St.

Atlanta, GA 30344

(678) 601-5580

www.atlfamilyimmigrationlaw.com

Testimonials

"I am a fellow lawyer but do not practice family law. I referred a mutual client to Judy to handle a very complicated custody matter on extremely short notice. Judy handled the case for my client like a champion and was communicative throughout the case with both me and the client. She not only won the case but truly knocked this complicated, convoluted custody and family violence matter OUT OF THE PARK, including an award of attorney's fees for her/my client. I would recommend Judy for every Georgia family law client going forward. Her team is amazing, and their customer service is A++!"

— Sarah

****

"Man my BM wouldn't let me see my daughter for over a year and Atty Delus got me joint custody, visitation, and worked on child support being super reasonable. Man she wasn't playing with my baby mom. Hire her for sure."

— Anonymous

****

"I was very satisfied with Attorney Judith's representation of my case. She was very professional from the moment I came to her office. I was fully informed of everything that was going on with my case. Also, her masterful articulation of the facts and closing arguments were at the highest level. Will highly recommend her to anyone that needs an attorney's service."

—Elijah

****

"Great, honest, and answered all of my questions. Very helpful."

—Anonymous

****

TABLE OF CONTENTS

ABOUT THE AUTHOR

My name is Judith Delus Montgomery, I have been practicing since about 2009, and I am an immigrant. I was born in Freeport, Bahamas, and came to the States at the age of four as an immigrant, to immigrant parents who are of Haitian descent.

Every member of my family has gone through the immigration process in some form or fashion. Thus, I grew up being very interested in immigration, how immigration works, and helping my family as a first-generation person in the United States in assimilating into American culture.

There were a lot of things that I, as an English speaker, would have to assist my family with.

I offered assistance in completing forms, going to the bank, opening business accounts, and starting their businesses. What's more, I played a significant role in assisting them with just about everything as it related to legal documents.

I had a desire very early on in immigration to assist those that didn't have a voice. So, my passion for immigration grew through that experience, especially since family law is very interesting. It's something that I began to really hone in on, and I realized that I was building a practice more in alignment with folks who are in couples where one of the spouses is a US citizen and one of the spouses is an immigrant. So, I've built this niche area by happenstance really, but I've been doing it for over ten years now, and it's something that I'm very proud of.

Many people call to speak with me and schedule a meeting because they want to understand what the ramifications are if a divorce happens while an immigration petition is pending. I felt that there weren't any books out there that touched on this subject.

Folks in my industry will typically either practice family law or immigration because they don't see how the two fields intersect, but I do. I have been invited to speak at different conferences, specifically the family law conference, to talk to family law lawyers about how family law and immigration intersect. I think that people are starting to get a handle or a better understanding of why these two areas of the law make sense.

That's the reason why I want to write this book. This book is for both US citizens that are married to immigrants, and immigrants that are married to US citizens -- so that they can understand what the law entails, and what the ramifications are when a marriage doesn't work out.

The US citizen spouse is the one who petitioned for you. Not only that they petitioned for you, but they're also your financial sponsor, and they made a promise to the US government that they would be responsible for you until such time that you can become a US citizen on your own accord, or for at least ten years. So, that's really what and who this book is for.

CHAPTER 1

COMMON ISSUES FACED BY IMMIGRANTS IN A DIVORCE

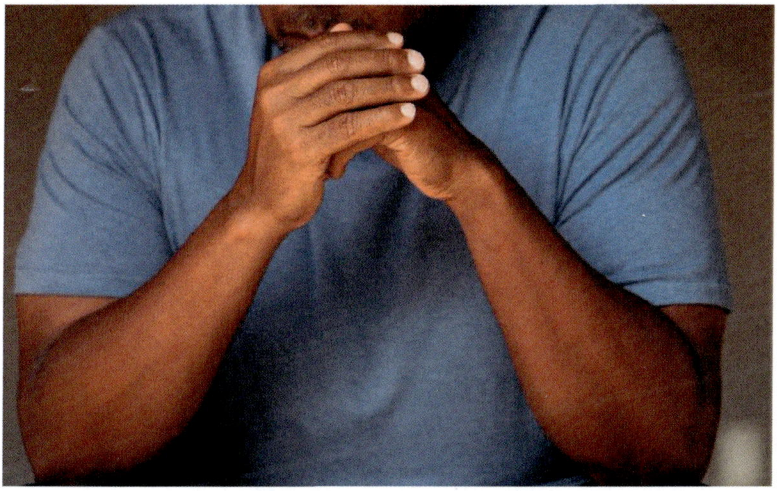

United States Customs and Immigration Services (USCIS) do not view divorce as an automatic indicator that the marriage was a sham. But be prepared that it will raise eyebrows with USCIS.

Just this morning, I met with a US citizen spouse who wanted to know if they could move forward with the divorce right away, if they needed to wait, or if they needed to sign a petition to assist their spouse in removing conditions from their green card. Their concern was about what it meant for them if they didn't sign the document.

The document in question is referred to as I 751, and it is the waiver to remove the conditions from the green card. The spouse is trying to decide if she should go ahead and sign, or if she can move forward with her divorce, and if she does move forward with her divorce, how it's going to affect her immigrant spouse.

The advice I gave was as follows: "If you're signing that document to remove the conditions on the green card, then you're telling the US government that the marriage is still intact, that you guys live together, have built a life together, that the rent or the mortgage is in both of your names, utilities are in both of your names, insurance is in both of your names, etc."

Here's the issue, these folks have been separated for several months and have not even lived together, and it sounds like they are intending to making false statements to USCIS.

This is a common question I get in my line of work.

My client and I had a very real conversation where I had to say, "You do understand that by signing this document, you're stating the marriage is intact. But not only that; this is going to be followed by an in-person interview where both parties are going to have to appear and give testimony under oath. You'll have to repeat those statements that you made in the documents, and you're going to have to be able to show proof of all the things that they are requesting." This was something she said she could not do.

If you can't do that, then you cannot sign that document. So the question then became, "How does this affect his standing in the United States?"

The immigrant spouse will have to seek out a waiver of the joint filing requirement and provide evidence that the marriage was in good faith when they entered into the marriage. Additionally, if he feels that he was abused in any way -- and abuse comes in many different forms, from physical to financial. Then his immigration attorney can argue those things or some other hardship or mistreatment that caused the breakdown of the marriage, then he may be able to move forward with a petition without her assistance. But, of course, this is just an example and it may not apply to every petition.

CHAPTER 2

MARRIAGES FAILING WHEN IMMIGRATION IS IN LIMBO

It is very common for marriages to fail while an immigration petition is in limbo, and I've built my practice in assisting individuals to overcome these hurdles.

At the onset of a relationship, there's a lot of love in the air. During the honeymoon phase when you're traveling back and forth, it's very romantic. You put your best foot forward when the person is coming to your country to visit with you and spend time. But that's very different from living with somebody every single day. So, sometimes you will see things fall apart pretty quickly once the parties move in together, and the real issues of life come into play.

There are several reasons the relationship can fall apart – but the most significant challenges tend to be financial.

When a US Citizen petitions for their immigrant partner to come to the United States, the immigrant partner is not legally authorized to work in the United States. Therefore, as part of the sponsorship, the US Citizen partner is agreeing to be financially responsible for their immigrant partner.

So, you have to be prepared to not only provide for yourself and for whatever else you have going on, but you must be able to juggle all of those things in addition to the needs of your new immigrant partner – without any governmental assistance.

This can significantly weigh on the USC partner and can sometimes place a significant burden on the relationship. Therefore, it is important to understand the ramifications of bringing over an immigrant partner to the United States.

CHAPTER 3

IMMIGRATION PROCESS IN MARRIAGE

If you have watched the popular show, 90 Day Fiancé, you probably have an idea of how this process goes. Here is a refresher:

The parties meet either on vacation or online, which then leads to dating and then they start considering a committed relationship that is followed by marriage. The parties want to be in the same country together and have chosen the United States. In that case, they can start the process with a K-1 visa which is the fiancé visa, where the US citizen applies for the non-immigrant to come to the United States for approximately ninety (90) days.

During this period, they will get to spend one-on-one time with each other, spend some time living together, getting to know one another, and seeing if things really work. Then, they go about getting married, for which they only have 90 days.

Most people who do this in real life decide to get married, even if they do not necessarily get along or they have not ironed out all their issues - very much like the show. Still, they feel like they can overcome it, and so they file the initial forms known as the I-485 Adjustment of Status Petition.

In the initial forms, you're going to need certain documentation, first and foremost, that marriage license. You're going to need the stamp that you entered into the United States legally or with inspection, and then there's going to be a whole host of other documents that you will need to support your marriage.

However, before you do that, there's a form known as the I-130 Relative Petition that needs to be filed and approved.

If you're married to a US citizen spouse, then you can file the I-130 and the I-485 concurrently – as long as both parties are in the United States. If the party is not a US citizen, but they are a green card holder, or if one party is not in the US, then they would file an I-130 first and wait for the approval.

Once the I-130 is approved, you will file the I-485 Adjustment of Status petition along with all the supporting documents that go along with that petition.

Once you have put all that together, paid the filing fee, completed a medical examination (you have the option to complete the medical examination before filing or before coming to the interview), and submitted it to USCIS, you will get what's called a receipt letter in the mail. This first document that you receive from USCIS will show that they have received your packet and it is being processed.

Then, in following months, the first thing that you will probably get will be the approval of the work permit authorization form that will allow an immigrant spouse to go and seek employment. In addition to that, it allows the immigrant spouse to get a social security card, and they can now go out and apply for a driver's license.

This is an exciting time for an immigrant who has been solely dependent on their USC spouse. It makes them feel like once they can work, they can drive, they can really get out here and maneuver on their own since they're now here in the US legally working and making a living and probably can provide for their families back in their home country.

The next notification you will receive from USCIS will be a biometrics appointment. This is where they will have to go in and get their fingerprints taken. Additionally, USCIS may capture different information to determine the identity of the parties. USCIS is verifying and confirming that you are who you say you are, that there's no fraud involved, and that there's no prior criminal record involved.

After the biometrics, most of my clients' petitions are processing within thirteen (13) months on average. At that point, hopefully, you are still together, happily married, and we can move forward with the in-person interview.

Once the couple attends the interview together, they answer all of the officer’s questions, verify the evidence provided, and ensure that the supporting documents are accurate. Then, the parties can consider that their petition will more than likely be approved.

So, your immigrant spouse will now have what's called a conditional green card. A conditional green card is only good for two years, and during those two years, it’s really an opportunity for USCIS to determine the validity of the marriage. Unfortunately, it is during those first two years that things typically start to fall apart.

Chapter 4

Obligations Of The Petitioner

The forms required are the family sponsorship form (I130), Supplemental Information Form (I130A), Green Card Application Form (I485), and Financial Support Form (I864).

The USC Spouse, once they submit that petition, they are saying that they are financially responsible for this person in every form or fashion. Whatever their needs are, they are to provide financially for that person. That is their obligation, and it's also an obligation when they submit the sponsorship petition that they are affirming responsibility for this person for the next ten years, or until that person becomes a US citizen on their own.

If anything happens before that, as in, they decide to go and seek out assistance from the government, then the USC spouse could be on the hook to the US government for any monetary amounts that they deem to be appropriate.

For example, if the person is getting public housing, food stamps, Social Security, or anything that had to be subsidized by the government because the USC spouse was not providing for that person, they could be responsible for reimbursing these government payouts.

However, most of the clients that I represent want to be in the United States because of the opportunities available, and the ability to find employment and be independent. Really, they want to just have the opportunity to find a job and get an education. They're often uninterested in staying home and being cared for by someone else, and it's quite honestly very uncomfortable for them to have to go through that process, to be completely and solely dependent on another human being which can also cause conflict.

The Rights Of The Immigrant Spouse

Immigrant spouses have the right to be in the United States legally and be married to their American spouses. Those are the rights they have when the petition first goes in. They do not have any other rights to work, obtain a driver's license, or get a social security card. They wouldn't be expected to file taxes because they don't have employment but if they have been working then they will need to show proof that they filed taxes each year they worked. Additionally, they have the right, like any typical citizen or resident, not to be mistreated, enslaved, or abused.

CHAPTER 5

WHAT TO EXPECT AT THE 90-DAY MARK

At the 90-day mark, those with the K-1 visa must be married. However, some situations are different and an immigrant spouse comes to the United States after having already married their US citizen spouse.

If they got married in the other country and then they came over, which happens, they kind of bypass the 90-day process. At the two-year mark, they need to submit the same waiver to remove the conditions from their green card so they can go from a two-year green card to a ten-year green card.

During this time, there is still an opportunity to report your immigrant spouse to USCIS for potential marriage fraud if you suspect that to be the case. I have had clients withdraw their support right before or at the interview when they had proof of fraud in their marriage. This ensured they would not be financially responsible for their immigrant spouse any longer.

Now, there are some immigrant spouses who come to the United States already having a 10-year green card, and if they're able to show that they have already surpassed the two-year mark, meaning if they've been married more than two years, usually, there is no waiting period and a 10-year green card will be immediately issued.

I've had potential clients call me about there being potential fraud in their marriage during this phase of the relationship. The thing is, if you've been married to someone for over three years, and they have been in another country for those three years, you may wonder what they've been doing.

So, it's interesting to me that people are willing to marry somebody and wait several years before the person comes to the US, and then later contact my office regarding a claim for fraud. This is not to say every marriage where parties remain apart for so long is fraud. But trust me when I say, I have seen it all. During those three years, new girlfriends, and even new babies have crept up.

Why Are Many People Not Surprised At The Time And Effort It Takes To Become A US Citizen By Marriage?

Many potential clients that call my office have already done a significant amount of research before they ever call. I would dare say a few of my clients know the process better than some paralegals. They know what hoops they will have to go through or overcome from friends or family members who have gone through the immigration process and can tell them exactly what it entails.

I don't find that most people are surprised. However, this is not to say that some people are not. Many USC spouses initiating the process are surprised by the length of time it takes for USCIS to process their partner's petition, but most people already know before they call me what the process is going to entail.

What's more interesting is that every administration is different. During the Obama administration, immigration attorneys were assured that petitions were being processed within normal timeframes. And much of the population felt confident in their own abilities to file immigration petitions with an attorney. However, things slowed down significantly under the Trump administration because petitions moved quicker for some countries – while other countries took forever, or didn't progress at all. Mostly because of racial biases by the administration. Currently under the Biden Administration processing of petitions has picked up but there are still immigration policies put in place by prior Administrations that are causing continued delays.

One thing I have learned during my decade of being a family immigration attorney is that legal counsel is still very much needed as individuals go through the process of obtaining status in the US.

CHAPTER 6

WHAT IF ONE SPOUSE IS SOLELY GIVEN CONTROL OF ALL FUNDS?

Could you imagine moving to a new country where you weren't familiar with the language; didn't have any family or friends; and couldn't make your own money and support yourself?

This process causes a lot of financial abuse where you hear people struggling and trying to fend for themselves because their USC spouse isn't supporting them financially.

Sometimes, individuals are even brought over to the US to be more a slave than a spouse. It's unfortunate to say this, but a lot of it is modern-day slavery where they believe that the immigrant spouse should be grateful to them that they were able to get here to the United States.

So for that reason, USC spouses feel that they can mistreat immigrant spouses. This is especially true because most times it's men who are bringing over female spouses from different countries and they believe that these women are going to be more submissive to them than American women.

Some USC spouses bring immigrant spouses over here with the belief that they're going to cook, clean, take care of their home, take care of them, and not go to work. So, that's where we see most of the issues begin. But then, very frequently, that financial abuse is also coupled with physical abuse.

It causes a lot of issues for a lot of young marriages that haven't built that firm foundation. It puts a lot of stress on new marriages when you find that you are solely responsible for the other person and you don't feel like they're pulling their weight. But you should go into it knowing that they're not going to be pulling their weight for quite some time, and you as the USC spouse should be in a financial position to take care of them. If you're not in a financial position to take care of your immigrant spouse, then maybe you should leave them alone.

CHAPTER 7

SCENARIOS THAT LEAD TO DETERIORATION OF MARRIAGES

I remember a client telling me that her USC spouse would clean his gun in front of her every day while he was looking at her, and sometimes he would point it at her while she was washing the dishes in the kitchen as a scare tactic. In another instance, I saw stepchildren causing the deterioration of new and fragile marital bonds. I sometimes see that people who have children allow their children to have a say in their relationship, and this can bring down a marriage very quickly if the parties don't get along.

I have a client that I'm working with right now whose adult children are making life a complete hell for the immigrant spouse, and it's very sad when you hear some of what is going on in those sorts of relationships.

There have been times when children have gotten physically violent with the immigrant spouse and the immigrant spouse was too afraid to call the police and file a police report because of their immigration status.

But anyone facing abuse should remember that you have rights in this country – and that physical abuse should never be tolerated. What's more, this form of abuse can open other avenues for you to seek status in the US either by way of a U Visa or VAWA.

The U nonimmigrant status (U visa) is set aside for victims of certain crimes who have suffered mental or physical abuse and are helpful to law enforcement or government officials in the investigation or prosecution of criminal activity.

The Violence Against Women Act (VAWA) creates and supports comprehensive, cost-effective responses to domestic violence, sexual assault, dating violence, and stalking.

These are the additional options I mentioned previously that an immigration attorney can file in support of abuse claims for their clients.

How And When Should Someone Notify Immigration Of A Divorce?

Immediately upon filing for divorce you should let immigration know. I say as soon as possible that the petitioner/sponsor will not be for very much longer.

It might be a good idea to attach a cover letter requesting that your initial joint petition be amended and changed into a divorce-based waiver.

You can also file an entirely new I-751 petition. Indeed, there is no legal limit on the number of I-751 petitions a person may file—although you should keep in mind that, practically speaking, submitting multiple filings could confuse immigration officers and, therefore, delay the adjudication of your case.

In either situation, consider also explaining the circumstances of your divorce, with evidence of your attempts to save your marriage, to strengthen your good faith marriage claim.

CHAPTER 8

HOW SOON AFTER FILING FOR DIVORCE ONE CAN EXPECT IMMIGRATION TO CONTACT

USCIS doesn't move very fast. It could be several months or years before you're contacted once the I-751 waiver is filed. During the time that you are waiting for a response, that is your opportunity to update them on any new information surrounding your divorce.

I'll give you a scenario where a client came to me after his divorce attorney botched his case severely and caused significant delays in his immigration matter.

Essentially, the attorney missed the final divorce hearing, and the judge signed an order that the marriage was not in good faith and that the US citizen spouse was entitled to all of her fees back that she had paid towards his immigration process.

It made things look very bad. And, unfortunately, he did not know about the divorce hearing. Had he known, he would have absolutely shown up, given testimony, and given his side of the story. But because he wasn't notified, he now has to explain to USCIS the reason for this ruling that could cause his immigration status to end.

My staff had to do a lot of research and digging, but the client was able to provide the information that showed proof of honesty on his part and a good faith marriage – and that the statements made by the USC spouse to the divorce court were not actually true.

Then, my firm filed a new I-751 waiver with USCIS, and we are currently awaiting an interview date. In the meantime, my client's green card status has been extended every 18 months, they have been able to remain in the United States, and they remain gainfully employed.

What Must Be Proven As The Immigrant Spouse

The immigrant spouse must prove that the marriage was in good faith. This can be accomplished through evidence in the form of pictures, videos, text messages, and more.

If you can prove that this marriage was in good faith, that it was not based on fraud, and that it was not with the intention of getting status in the United States, then you're probably going to be able to overcome the divorce and be allowed to obtain a 10-year green card.

Red Flags That Immigration Is Looking For When They See A Divorce

Anything under two years is going to be a red flag, which is the point of putting in that condition because USCIS wants to see what's going to happen in those two years.

Immediate red flags for USCIS are: parties never lived together or had the same address; parties don't have a signed lease agreement, there is a difference in shared language or religion; there is no shared bank account; there is no shared car insurance coverage; there is no shared health insurance or life insurance. And most importantly, when the petitioner fails to appear for the USCIS interview, it is an alarming sign for immigration officials.

The Evidence Needed To Prove That The Marriage Was In Good Faith

Affidavits from family that were present during the courting phase are a good start.

During the courting phase, if you have people who are with you and interacted with you as a couple and attended the wedding day, this is very strong evidence.

Evidence of shared financial responsibility, joint bank accounts, joint credit cards, lease agreements, car insurance, and health insurance to name a few. Creating life together (i.e. having a child) is an even stronger indication of the parties' intention to be together for 18 years or more.

You'll also need your tax returns to show that you've been paying taxes, or that you're on a payment plan if you maintained employment. You'll have to show employee verification if you're the US citizen spouse, and that you can afford to provide for yourself and your new spouse. You can even submit your passport stamps when you visited each other. The more the proof, the better, because USCIS doesn't like to see gaps.

During the time that you are dating from afar, the parties must visit each other -- usually, at least once within the last two years. USCIS is less inclined to approve anything where you haven't seen this person in two or three years.

During the pandemic, when many borders were closed, it has been difficult for many couples to see each other. As more countries are beginning to learn to live with COVID-19, couples can now resume visiting each other.

The Importance of Financial Support From USC Spouse

A USC Spouse will sign an affidavit of support (USCIS Form I-864) for the immigrant spouse, as is required in all family-based immigration cases. This means that the signer accepts legal responsibility for providing financial support until one of four things happen:

1. The immigrant spouse dies,
2. The immigrant spouse becomes a U.S. citizen,
3. The immigrant spouse accrues 40 work quarters credited toward Social Security (approximately ten years), or
4. The immigrant spouse permanently leaves the United States.

Divorce, as you will notice, is not on that list. Indeed, divorce does not terminate your financial responsibilities toward your immigrant spouse.

Whether you will be on the hook for financial support depends on whether your Affidavit has already been submitted to the U.S. government, and on whether your spouse's application for permanent residence ultimately gets approved. If it's still early in the process, you should write to USCIS to withdraw your I-130 Petition for Alien Relative as soon as possible, then refuse to supply the I-864 and any other requested documents, so that final green-card approval does not go through.

If, however, all application materials are in and your immigrant spouse has already been approved for conditional or permanent residence, it's probably too late to back out. The only way USCIS is likely to undo your spouse's grant of a green card, and therefore your support obligation, is if it was obtained through fraud. But if that's the case, and you were aware of possible fraud then you might also be implicated in the scheme, and could face penalties.

Depending on How Early Your Petition is in the Process, This Could Impact Your Immigration Status

As an example, if a marriage was based on fraud, that could truly impact your immigration case. But if it was irreconcilable differences, not as much. Even adultery doesn't matter; adultery means that the person was a cheater, not so much that the marriage was based on fraud.

If the I-130 immigrant petition is still pending before USCIS, the agency ultimately won't approve it – assuming the USC Spouse writes in to advise of the situation and withdraws their petition.

Or, if the I-130 has already been approved but the case is awaiting an interview at a U.S. consulate or a USCIS office within the United States, the government officials handling the case will ask enough questions to uncover the divorce and deny the case at that time.

If the immigrant spouse is living in the U.S. with no other legal immigration status at the time of the denial, USCIS is likely to issue a Notice to Appear (NTA). This will initiate removal (deportation) proceedings in immigration court.

What To Do If You Are A USC Spouse And Victim Of Fraud

If you married someone whom you later come to suspect was merely using you as a path to a U.S.

green card, you might want to file a tip with USCIS or Immigration and Customs Enforcement (ICE).

The U.S. government has the power to initiate an investigation and ultimately place the immigrant in deportation (removal) proceedings. With fraud on record, your (presumably ex-) immigrant spouse would likely never again be able to receive a U.S. visa or green card.

However, consider whether USCIS or ICE might have grounds upon which to suspect that you were complicit in the sham marriage. You would not want to file a tip only to become the target of an investigation. If it goes the wrong way, you could conceivably face fines and other criminal penalties.

Also, consider whether you have enough convincing evidence to persuade the government to follow up on your tip. They receive lots of these tips, and many in the past have turned out to be attempted revenge by U.S. citizen spouses who felt betrayed after a marriage fell apart – even if the marriage truly was entered into in good faith on both sides.

Still, a possible reason to file such a tip is that, in order to get your spouse's initial green card application approved, you had to sign an I-864 promising to financially maintain your non-citizen spouse. It is legally unclear whether you, as a duped spouse, could successfully argue that your responsibility under the I-864 should be ended.

As mentioned earlier, divorce by itself will not terminate a petitioner's obligations under the Affidavit of Support. However, these obligations would definitely end if your ex were to lose the green card and leave (or be deported from) the United States.

What To Do If Your Spouse's Allegations Are Untrue

If they are untrue, that means the immigrant spouse will have proof to contest that the allegations aren't true. What I have learned in over a decade of doing immigration law, is that immigrant spouses do a very good job of collecting evidence to support their petition for USCIS consideration.

So, during conversations parties know nothing about, the immigrant spouse may be recording you. Also, text messages while dating, emails, love letters, trips and vacations, videos, and pictures from the wedding are all very helpful to support or deny a claim of fraud against you.

Filing police reports for later proof is another good form of supporting evidence. If you had to file temporary protective orders in court, that evidence goes a long way. Having proof of ongoing abuse through the relationship is very strong supporting evidence as well.

Protections Outside Of An Immigration Petition In Cases Of Abuse

One of the major protections that the USCIS provides is through a program called VAWA.

A VAWA petition is Violence Against Women and Children. Even though it says women and children, (who are the most common survivors of domestic issues), men can also use VAWA as a way to obtain status in the United States.

I have discussed supporting evidence at length above. So, just make sure to have your evidence to support your petition for abuse and violence.

All is not lost if you do not have police reports, because immigration understands that in an abusive situation, it may not be easy to call the police on someone you love - even though they are hurting you. And again, family and friends' affidavits will assist if an immigrant spouse is unable to move forward with their initial marital petition, and the Violence Against Women Act of 1994 can be a significant tool as well.

This range of protections was extended to same-sex couples and battered undocumented immigrants so that they could claim temporary visas, but VAWA is one of them, and the other one is a U-Visa.

A U-visa just has to do with crimes against a non-immigrant. So if you know the person who committed a crime against you, or you're able to help the police bring this person to justice, that will help you as well. So, if you've been a victim of criminal activity, and you have suffered either physical abuse or mental abuse, then you could petition for a U-visa.

CHAPTER 9

WHAT IF THE PARTIES ARE IN THE PROCESS OF IMMIGRATION AND DIVORCE AND THERE ARE CHILDREN IN THE RELATIONSHIP?

Being an immigrant going through a divorce doesn't change what happens in the divorce. Your immigration status should not factor into the court's decision unless the immigrant spouse is considering returning to their home country with their children.

If you retained my firm, we would ask for alimony and child support (if children are born of the marriage). If you are the victim of abuse, we'll be asking for some sort of support because more times than not, if your status is pending and you haven't worked or you've been pregnant and having babies, you probably weren't able to work. So, you're going to need some sort of financial support, especially with minor children.

So when we petition for your divorce, we're going to be asking for those things and outline that the US citizen spouse brought the immigrant spouse to the United States and they have been the sole provider for the immigrant spouse and the minor children and therefore remains responsible for them.

We will then generally argue that support should continue until such time that the immigrant spouse can get on their feet and become employed.

Receiving Alimony Or Spousal Support As A US Immigrant Without Citizenship

Family law cases have nothing to do with immigration court. For example, I represented an immigrant client who didn't have any status, but he wanted visitation and joint custody of his children, and he now has visitation and joint custody of his children.

You're entitled to alimony if you need it, you're entitled to child support if you need it, you're entitled to visitation, and you're entitled to joint legal custody. Your rights are no less than anyone else's just because you don't have status in the United States.

Still, the USC spouse tends to feel that they have an upper hand because they're the American. So, we have to be vigilant on behalf of the immigrant spouse to ensure the court is going to uphold the rights of all parties that walk into their courtroom.

The best interest of the child is the standard all courts use in a divorce proceeding. Therefore, they will ensure the child(ren) have stability, continuity, support, and both parents in their lives. If alimony and child support is needed to ensure that occurs, then it will be granted.

How Assets Are Divided During A Divorce

During a divorce proceeding, some courts require parties to complete a Domestic Relations Financial Affidavit (DRFA) to determine the assets and liabilities of the parties. Additionally, all possessions obtained during the marriage are fair game for both parties. This includes: real property, vehicles, jewelry, credit cards, and taxes.

The divorce court will be able to ascertain who has been the breadwinner in the marriage and how best to support the person who was not working. If the immigrant spouse hasn't been working, and if they have been the responsibility of the US citizen spouse, then a division of assets or debts incurred during the marriage will probably go in favor or towards the US citizen. They will probably be able to keep the assets that they acquired prior to marriage, but they're going to have to help their immigrant spouse acquire a new place to live and financial support - even if only for a temporary amount of time.

The courts are going to try to make it as fair as possible. They don't want one party coming into the court with an upper hand. So, if the immigrant spouse doesn't have the funds to pay for an attorney, then the USC spouse will have to chip in so everyone is properly represented.

Both parties are entitled to the same representation. The person that has been responsible for that immigrant spouse will need to also pay the attorney's fees. Parties don't realize that, but that's pretty common.

So I say, the best way to keep the courts out of your personal affairs is by coming to an agreement with each other in writing beforehand and having a family attorney (like my firm) draft all the documents for you and file an uncontested divorce. Otherwise, a person wearing a black robe will determine who gets what and you both may not like their ultimate decision.

CHAPTER 10

WHAT IF YOU AND YOUR US SPOUSE ARE SEPARATING, NOT DIVORCING?

Not all States acknowledge a separation. However, Georgia does have legal separation. Which very much looks like a divorce. The issues and processes are identical. The only difference is the parties have not decided to officially cut ties.

If you're separating, what does that mean? Does that mean that you guys are living in different locations? Does that mean that you guys have separated your bank accounts? Does that mean that you are no longer on their health insurance, their life insurance, or their car insurance?

If it means living separate lives, you have something to worry about because you're not married and building a life together. For immigration purposes, this will cause you issues.

There are specific questions that will be asked of you at the interview and under oath, you have a duty to tell the truth. There is specific evidence and documentation that has to be submitted, and if you're not living together, then you can't submit those documents.

If you can't submit those documents, then you don't really have a marriage. And if you do not have a marriage on which your immigration petition is based, then you are generally not entitled to the benefits under that petition.

What An Immigrant Spouse Can Do To Prepare Themselves Heading Towards A Divorce

Most folks are already building their case, and often, they'll come to the firm and say they have significant evidence.

If you have the evidence listed in previous chapters, then that's the evidence that we need. However, there are rarely police reports since immigrants generally do not trust the police, so they will not report the abuse.

(The reason I continue to mention abuse is because that is usually the reason for most divorces that come to my firm. This is generally the breakdown for most marriages.)

To many immigrants, America has become anti-immigrant over the years. Therefore, immigrants do not trust the police to act in their best interest. They don't trust that the police will protect them, and they believe that their status is so fragile in the United States that if they do call in, the police will end up contacting ICE who will then place them into deportation proceedings.

For that reason, most of them will not contact the police. So, even with no police report, you have to understand and believe that there has been abuse, and someone probably has seen the abuse or witnessed the abuse, so we would need an affidavit from them. Remember, phone video recording is a great resource.

Chapter 11

When To Hire An Immigration Attorney

Yesterday! As soon as you have made up your mind to divorce, it is time to hire an attorney. Especially, if you have sponsored an immigrant and that I-864 has been approved, we have to work fast.

Potential clients call my office all the time because they want us to sway them in one direction or not. That's not what we do. We don't sway you in the direction of a divorce. That has to be a decision that you, and you alone can make. But once you have made that decision, then you need to give us a call, and we're going to help you make the best decision to move forward with your life whether you are the USC spouse or the immigrant spouse.

How An Attorney Can Help Clients Through The Divorce Process As Well As The Immigration Investigation Process

Based on years of experience and handling different cases, you are in good hands at my firm. Since I've seen so many different kinds of cases, my team and I know how to jump through the USCIS hoops gracefully.

I'm able to strategize and come up with how you should go about handling your case —depending on which side of the ball you stand on. So, because I've done it each way, I know what it's like to represent a USC spouse, and I know what it's like to represent an immigrant spouse.

With that experience and knowledge, we're able to properly prepare the client and articulate their needs to USCIS, NVC, or the courts so that our clients can be successful.

But the fact that I specifically have the experience of doing a divorce from beginning to close, and handling immigration cases from beginning to close, that's what makes my firm the best candidate for the job.

There isn't too much that I haven't seen. It could be I'm a little bit jaded, but what I can say is that I know both areas of law very well, and can walk you through and strategize how to move forward while both cases are processing concurrently. Most attorneys only handle just family law or just immigration law. We are a one-stop shop and can handle both.

Lastly, I am not just a family/immigration attorney but I am also a naturalized citizen. That means I have been through the immigration process and can not only sympathize but also empathize with what you are going through. This enables my firm and I to show compassion in the work that we do for our clients. Legal fees can get very expensive so you must land at the correct firm that will prioritize you as an individual.

If you find that we're not representing a client in both cases concurrently, it is because they have chosen that the legal fees are a bit high for them to have us represent them in two separate matters, and they've chosen to go with one case first, and then once they're done with that case, they will retain us for the second case.

It happens all the time. But our position is that we can get you to the other side of this with either a green card or ultimately citizenship if you've already gotten your green card. If we're going through the side of the USC spouse, then we know how to minimize any sort of alimony, and we know how to minimize the financial burden that may fall upon you. However, this does not apply to child support; child support cannot be waived by either party and is a requirement in place to protect any minor children of the relationship.

What Is The Next Step?

Give us a call at (678) 601-5580 or visit www.atlfamilyimmigrationlaw.com. You can schedule a case evaluation meeting with one of my team members to further discuss your legal options. We look forward to hearing from you soon!

Index

V

W

NOTES

Made in the USA
Coppell, TX
11 November 2026

11803122R00045